DC BATMAN & ROBIN

THE SPITTING IMAGE

Batman and Robin Use DNA Analysis to Crack the Case

by Steve Korté
art by Dario Brizuela
Batman created by Bob Kane with Bill Finger

Consultants:
David Foran, PhD, and Zachariah Landhuis, BA
Michigan State University
Forensic Science Graduate Program
East Lansing, Michigan

CAPSTONE PRESS
a capstone imprint

Late at night, the Batmobile moves silently through the dark streets of Gotham City. Batman and Robin are on patrol, looking for any criminal activity.

Suddenly, they receive a message from the Gotham City Police Department.

"There has been a break-in at the Gotham Gems jewelry store on the corner of First Avenue and Cedar Street," says the police officer.

"That's just a few blocks from here," says Batman as he punches the gas on the Batmobile.

Batman and Robin rush to the jewelry store. The store looks completely dark, and its door is wide open.

"It looks like we arrived before the police," says Robin as he hops out of the Batmobile.

Batman steps through the door and tries to turn on the lights. When they don't work, he shines a flashlight on the store's security system.

"Someone cut the power and destroyed the security camera," Batman says. "Whoever broke in didn't want to be recorded."

Batman quickly restores the power. Bright lights fill the jewelry store.

"Batman!" Robin gasps. "Look over there!"

In the middle of the room stands a large glass display case with a jagged hole in one side. Shards of broken glass are scattered on the floor. The case is completely empty.

A few feet away, a man wearing a uniform lies sprawled on the floor. He softly groans in pain.

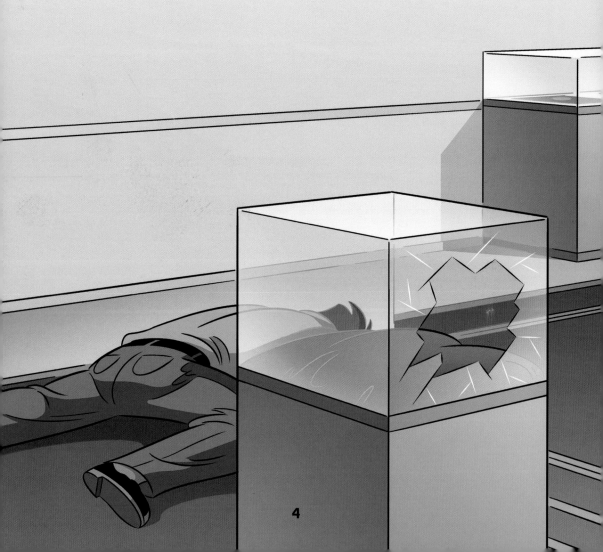

Robin carefully helps the man sit up.

"What . . . what happened?" asks the man.

"There's been a burglary here," says Batman. "What can you tell us?"

"I'm the store's security guard, and tonight I . . . ouch!"

The man pauses to gently touch a bright red bruise on his neck. Batman peers closely at the mark.

"That's a recent bruise," the Dark Knight says. "How did you get it?"

"Someone turned off the lights in the store tonight," says the guard. "I heard the sound of glass breaking. It was dark, so I couldn't see who did it. I tried to grab the person. We struggled for a while, and I felt myself being choked. Then I got knocked to the floor. I must have blacked out."

"And the thief got away with some jewels," says Robin.

"Can you tell us anything more about your fight with the thief?" asks Batman.

"Yes, I think so," says the guard. "While we were struggling, I heard the store's phone being knocked to the floor. Then the thief held onto me with one hand and used another hand to wrap something around my throat. That's all I can remember."

"Batman, I found the phone," says Robin.

"Don't touch it, Robin," says Batman. "We need to dust it for fingerprints."

Robin crouches down. He removes a small metal container and a brush from his Utility Belt. He then lightly brushes black powder onto both the telephone and the display case to search for fingerprints.

"No sign of any prints, Batman," says Robin.

"The thief probably wore gloves," replies Batman. "But there's a chance that the thief left behind another clue for us."

"You mean DNA?" asks Robin.

"Exactly," says Batman.

FACT
DNA stands for deoxyribonucleic acid. It is a material found in the cells of every living thing. DNA determines the characteristics of all organisms — from onions and oak trees to insects and humans.

"We need to look for any item in the store that might contain DNA from the thief," says Batman as he carefully searches the store.

"What should we be looking for?" asks Robin.

"Almost anything," says Batman. "Even if it's just a tiny flake of skin or a single drop of a body fluid, we can try to collect a DNA sample. Some criminal cases have been solved by the DNA found in a single strand of hair."

FACT

People leave behind DNA all the time without even thinking about it. Every day, the average person sheds 40 to 100 strands of hair and about 600,000 outer skin cells.

"Robin, I have a theory about this phone cord," says Batman. "I need you to collect it as evidence. Do you remember the procedure I taught you?"

Without speaking, Robin nods.

Robin removes his black gloves. Then he puts on a fresh pair of disposable latex gloves and pulls tweezers from his Utility Belt. The Boy Wonder carefully uses the tweezers to pick up the phone cord. He then places the cord inside a paper envelope.

"The police will be here soon to take a full report," Batman says, turning to the guard. "Please tell them that we are working on the case."

"Let's go, Robin," says Batman. "We have some lab work to do in the Batcave."

Soon, the Batmobile zooms through the streets of Gotham City. The Dynamic Duo head back to their secret underground headquarters.

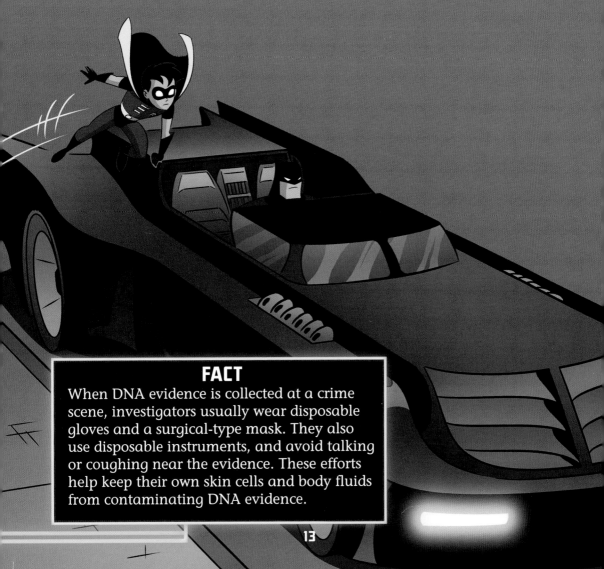

FACT
When DNA evidence is collected at a crime scene, investigators usually wear disposable gloves and a surgical-type mask. They also use disposable instruments, and avoid talking or coughing near the evidence. These efforts help keep their own skin cells and body fluids from contaminating DNA evidence.

Back at the Batcave, Robin hands Batman the envelope with the phone cord.

"So what's your theory about this cord?" asks Robin.

FACT

Investigators use paper envelopes or bags to collect DNA evidence. Biological evidence is not stored in plastic bags because plastic traps moisture, and the evidence rots. Paper allows the evidence to dry and breathe.

"The thief may have used one gloved hand to hold onto the guard and the other to wrap the phone cord around his throat," says Batman. "There's a chance that the thief put the other end of the phone cord in his or her mouth to keep the cord tight."

"That would explain the moisture on the cord!" says Robin.

"If there is saliva on one end of the telephone cord, we might be able to extract DNA from it," says Batman.

Robin looks doubtful. "But the cord is so thin," he says. "How are we going to get a sample from it?"

Batman nods. "You're right, Robin. If a sample is too small, it can be difficult to get a DNA profile. Fortunately, there is a process to make more than one billion copies of a single strand of DNA. I'll walk you through it after you suit up."

"There are several steps we need to do to analyze a DNA sample," says Batman.

"Can't we just look through the microscope to see the DNA?" asks Robin.

"Unfortunately, it's not that simple," says Batman. "We're going to be using chemicals and electricity to analyze the sample and create a DNA profile."

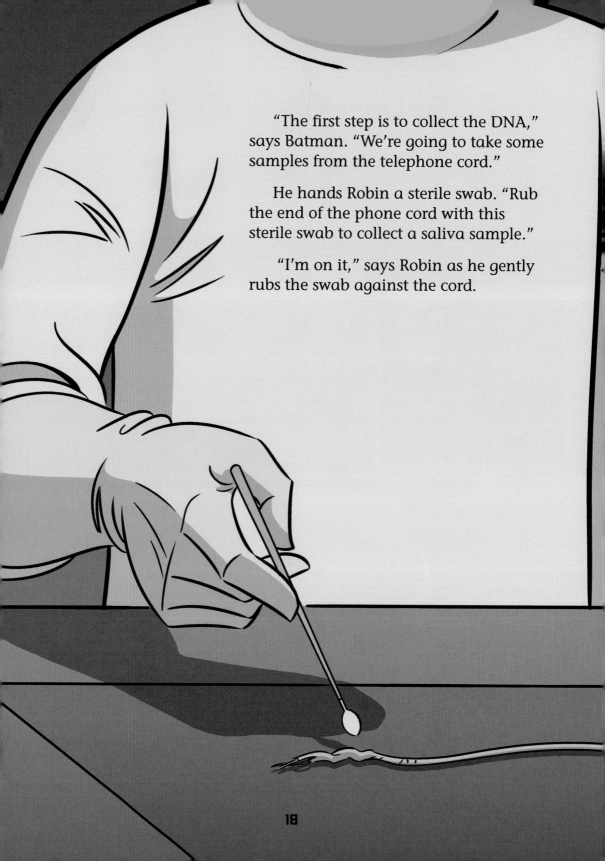

"The first step is to collect the DNA," says Batman. "We're going to take some samples from the telephone cord."

He hands Robin a sterile swab. "Rub the end of the phone cord with this sterile swab to collect a saliva sample."

"I'm on it," says Robin as he gently rubs the swab against the cord.

"Good work, Robin," says Batman. "Now place the cotton part of the swab into a small plastic tube. Then take a new swab and collect another sample. You'll do this a few times to make sure we get a good DNA sample."

Robin collects a few more samples. "I'm ready for the next step, Batman."

"Now we need to extract the DNA from those samples," says Batman. "We add a series of liquid chemicals to each tube using this pipette. Mix them thoroughly to break open the cells and release the DNA. Then place the tubes into a centrifuge."

"The final step is to create a DNA profile," says Batman. "This machine is called a genetic analyzer. It uses electricity to separate the different sections of copied DNA. The analyzer has a laser and camera that detects the DNA sections as they move, and the pattern that is created is printed out."

"You mean like a chart or a map?" asks Robin.

"Exactly," says Batman. "Each person's DNA results in a pattern that is unlike any other person's, except for identical twins. This analyzer will produce and show us those patterns."

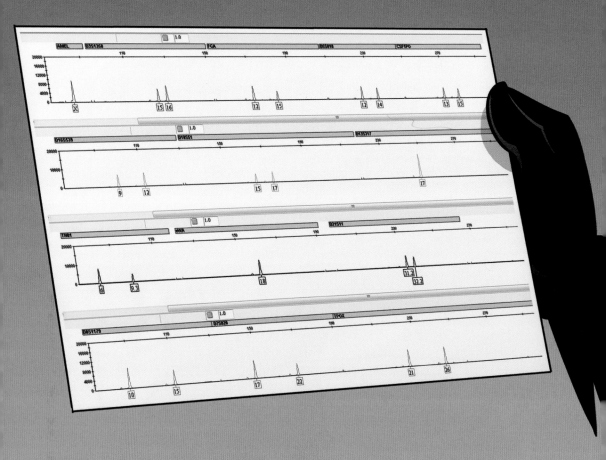

A short time later, Batman removes a piece of paper from the Batcomputer. It's covered with a series of lines in different colors.

"Take a look at these horizontal colored lines that go up and then down to form peaks," says Batman. "Do you see the patterns of those peaks? Each peak represents a section of DNA."

"That's the DNA profile of our suspect?" asks Robin.

"That's right," says Batman. "And if we can find an exact match for this profile, we will know whose DNA is on the telephone cord."

"Before we compare this profile to other ones in DNA databases from around the world, let's see what we can find here in Gotham City," says Batman.

"The city has its own DNA database?" asks Robin.

"Yes, the Gotham City Medical Examiner's office has been collecting DNA samples from crime scenes and convicted criminals for years," replies Batman.

GOTHAM CITY
MEDICAL
EXAMINER'S
OFFICE

FACT

Most countries maintain their own DNA databases. The United States' database is called the Combined DNA Index System (CODIS). It is the largest in the world. It contains millions and millions of DNA profiles.

Minutes later, Robin jumps out of his chair. "Batman, we have a match!" he says. "The Batcomputer found a database sample with the exact same DNA profile as the saliva sample from the jewelry store."

"You might even say it's a spitting image!" Robin adds with a grin.

Batman stares at the screen. "Catwoman," he says. "I might have known. Like most cats, she has a fondness for shiny objects."

"Luckily for us, this cat left her mark at the scene of the crime," says Robin.

Batman and Robin rush over to Catwoman's luxury apartment. They burst through the door, hoping to surprise her.

Catwoman is ready for them, though. She spins around and kicks her leg in the air. Her foot slams into Robin's chest.

As Robin tumbles to the floor, he crashes into Batman, knocking down the Dark Knight.

Catwoman smiles as she quickly grabs a large pile of jewels. She runs over to the window.

Batman grabs a Batrope from his Utility Belt and quickly throws it around Catwoman's waist. With a sharp tug, he pulls Catwoman off the window ledge.

She lands on the apartment floor with a thud. The jewels tumble onto the carpet.

"No more jewelry store shopping trips for you, Catwoman," says Batman.

"That's right," agrees Robin. "The only bracelets you're going to be wearing are these handcuffs."

MORE ABOUT DNA ANALYSIS

- DNA contains the basic chemical information that makes each person or living thing unique. DNA is found in every cell in our body except red blood cells. No two people have the same DNA, except identical twins.

- DNA was discovered in the late 1860s by a Swiss chemist named Friedrich Miescher. It wasn't until 1953 that three scientists, Francis Crick, James Watson, and Rosalind Franklin, were able to figure out the exact structure of DNA.

- A DNA profile is sometimes called a DNA fingerprint. In 1984, a British scientist named Alec Jeffreys was the first to use DNA fingerprinting to help the police solve a pair of murders.

- Actual fingerprints are used to identify unknown suspects 10 times more often than DNA evidence.

- In the early 1990s, Dr. Kary Mullis developed a method to create multiple copies of DNA. He doubled a small section of DNA. Those two DNA sections were then doubled again to make four copies, then eight, and then 16. By repeating the process 30 times, more than one billion identical copies were created.

- DNA evidence can sometimes solve crimes from hundreds of years ago. It all depends on whether the DNA was exposed to heat, moisture, sunlight, or oxygen. Any or all of those can destroy DNA molecules.

- DNA evidence isn't just used to prove someone committed a crime. The Innocence Project was formed in 1992. It has used DNA matching to overturn wrongful convictions for hundreds of people.

- DNA databases help the police catch people who commit crimes more than once. In 2013, 61 percent of DNA profiles found at crime scenes in England matched up with samples in the British criminal database.

GLOSSARY

analyze (AN-uh-lize)—to examine something carefully in order to understand it

centrifuge (SEN-tri-fyuj)—a machine that spins substances of different densities to separate them

contaminate (kuhn-TA-muh-nayt)—to make dirty or unfit for use

database (DAY-tuh-bays)—a collection of organized information, often on a computer

DNA (dee-en-AY)—material in cells that gives living things their individual characteristics; DNA stands for deoxyribonucleic acid

evidence (EV-uh-duhnss)—information, items, and facts that help prove something to be true or false

latex (LAY-teks)—a rubbery material that stretches

molecule (MOL-uh-kyool)—the atoms making up the smallest unit of a substance

profile (PROH-file)—a graph or other representation of information showing the particular characteristics of something

saliva (suh-LYE-vuh)—the clear liquid in your mouth that helps you swallow and begin to digest food

sterile (STER-uhl)—free of germs

theory (THEE-ur-ee)—an idea that explains something that is unknown

READ MORE

Anniss, Matt. *Criminal Profiling*. Crime Science. New York: Gareth Stevens Publishing, 2014.

Litmanovich, Ellina, and Sara L. Latta. *Investigating DNA and Blood*. Crime Scene Investigators. New York: Enslow Publishing, 2018.

Orr, Tamra B. *Investigating a Crime Scene*. Follow the Clues. Ann Arbor, Mich.: Cherry Lake Publishing, 2014.

INTERNET SITES

Use FactHound to find Internet sites related to this book.
Visit *www.facthound.com*
Just type in 9781515768586 and go.

INDEX

OTHER TITLES IN THIS SET

**FOOTWEAR &
TREAD ANALYSIS**

**FIRE
INVESTIGATION**

**FINGERPRINT
ANALYSIS**

Published by Capstone Press in 2017
1710 Roe Crest Drive
North Mankato, Minnesota 56003
www.mycapstone.com

Cataloging-in-publication information is on file with the Library of Congress.
ISBN 978-1-5157-6858-6 (library binding)
ISBN 978-1-5157-6871-5 (eBook PDF)

Editorial Credits
Christopher Harbo, editor; Brann Garvey, designer; Tori Abraham, production specialist

Summary: Batman and Robin use DNA analysis techniques to solve a burglary at the Gotham Gems
jewelry store.

Illustration Credits
Luciano Vecchio, back cover, 1, 32

Capstone and the author thank Katelyn Kranz, from the Michigan State University Forensic Science
Graduate Program, for supplying the DNA profile for Catwoman in this book.

Printed in the United States of America.
010364F17